DOUGHNUTS

DOUGHNUTS

OVER 3 DOZEN
CRULLERS, FRITTERS,
AND OTHER TREATS

DORIAN LEIGH PARKER

Illustrations by Sally Sturman

Clarkson Potter/Publishers
New York

TO MY FRIEND LEO LERMAN, FOR HIS
UNFAILING SUPPORT AND APPROVAL THROUGH MORE
THAN HALF A CENTURY . . . WITH LOVE

❧

Published by Clarkson N. Potter, Inc., 201 East 50th Street, New York, New
York 10022. Member of the Crown Publishing Group.
Random House, Inc. New York, Toronto, London, Sydney, Auckland
CLARKSON POTTER, POTTER, and colophon are trademarks of
Crown Publishers, Inc.

Manufactured in the United States of America

Design by Howard Klein

Library of Congress Cataloging-in-Publication Data
Parker, Dorian Leigh
Doughnuts: over 3 dozen crullers, fritters, and other treats
/ Dorian Leigh Parker
p. cm.
1. Doughnuts. I. Title.
TX770.D67P37 1994
641.8'653—dc20
ISBN 0-517-59439-0
10 9 8 7 6 5 4 3 2 1

First Edition

CONTENTS

∞

PREFACE

∽

Born in Texas of fiercely Southern antecedents, I was brought up on fried food: fried chicken, of course, as well as fried steak, pork chops, and veal cutlets, crisp fried eggplant and green tomatoes, fried sweet potatoes and chewy fried corn. For breakfast there often would be fried biscuits with preserves or squares of fried cornmeal mush with fried squirrel—my grandmother's favorite.

In self-defense I became a gourmand—a food-freak in current argot. As I traveled through life, and northward, I collected gastronomic knowledge while still retaining a taste for fried fare, which I learned to differentiate as sautéed, stir-fried, or deep-fried. At college in Virginia I appreciated the fried oysters and crab cakes, and fried Smithfield ham with fried apples at breakfast, but best of all, I discovered doughnuts!

After college I lived in Bucks County, Pennsylvania, where my day began with doughnuts delivered to my door by a Pennsylvania Dutch bakery. Seven years later I moved to France, where I learned to cook haute cuisine at the Cordon Bleu and "cuisine bonne femme" at home, with supplementary doughnut-making sessions when overcome by nostalgia.

One day I found, to my joy, a little stand under the Sacre Coeur where an enterprising ex-GI sold homemade yeast-raised doughnuts. I sent them by the boxful to my ten-year-old son at his posh Swiss school, thereby creating a body of young aesthetes with an appetite for American doughnuts, and establishing my son's popularity at the same time.

INTRODUCTION

∞

Twixt the optimist and pessimist
The difference is droll:
The optimist sees the doughnut
But the pessimist sees the hole.
MCLANDBURGH WILSON (C. 1915)

The *Encyclopaedia Britannica* says that the technique of frying is "ancient, ubiquitous, and versatile." This method of cooking developed logically wherever there was a supply of fat or oil. The kind of fat used for frying differed according to region: sesame and soybean oil in the Asian area, olive oil in the Mediterranean countries, and primarily animal fat in the northern reaches.

Fried foods were often prepared to commemorate various events or represent ideals. In ancient China, rings of fried sweet dough symbolized Eternity, and fried cakes found under the lava at Pompeii were made for funeral feasts to represent the cycle of life and death. In our own country, a petrified fried round of dough with a hole was unearthed on the site of a prehistoric tribe in existence before the Pueblos.

During the Middle Ages on Shrove Tuesday in northern Europe, fried cakes and pancakes were eaten just as they were by the Celts on All Hallows' Eve. In early British records of 1381 A.D., there appears a recipe for another fried delicacy, fritter batter: "Make thereto with flowere and fry hem with fresche grees." In the fifteenth century, almond fritters and elderberry funnel cakes were choice desserts, which now are best known as a specialty of our own Pennsylvania Dutch cooks.

The first fried cakes known as doughnuts were raised by barm or bakers' yeast, and the cake type came into being after the invention of baking powder in the nineteenth century. The choice between the two varieties is a matter of individual preference.

In 1920, Adolph Levitt invented a doughnut machine, setting the stage for the widespread doughnut shops of today. He stimulated the demand for his wares by putting the machine in the window of his store so that passersby could enjoy watching the production of the golden cakes, and then naturally wander in to sample one, and bring more home.

INGREDIENTS

Unbleached flour, unsalted butter, vegetable oil, and bulk yeast are recommended in all the recipes. Bulk yeast may be purchased at health-food stores. I have found it to be cheaper, fresher, and more potent than the commercially packaged yeast.

OILS

Before the word *cholesterol* entered the vocabulary of the general public, fried foods were part of every country's cookery, particularly their "street foods." The fish-and-chips of England rivaled the *pommes frites* of France, the egg rolls of China matched the tempura of Japan, and in each cuisine there was some form of sweetened fried dough as an irresistible treat.

Fat is divided into two categories: unsaturated and saturated. To generalize, vegetable oils are unsaturated and animal fat is saturated to varying degrees. The oil for frying can be selected from numerous unsaturated vegetable oils, including olive, canola or rapeseed, sunflower, corn, soybean, safflower, and peanut, which studies have determined to be more nutritionally sound than saturated fats.

COOKING UTENSILS

A thermometer that can be clipped to the side of the cooking vessel is crucial for monitoring the temperature of the oil and should be positioned on the pan before heating the oil. The pan should be heavy, with a steady bottom wide enough to allow the food to move freely. The sides of the pan should be high enough to accommodate the thermometer, and the oil must come no more than halfway up the sides of the pan. The pan may be heavy aluminum, stainless steel, or cast iron. There are also pans designed especially for frying and electric fryers that control the temperature by thermostat. A Chinese wok may also be used.

Other necessary utensils are a long-handled skimmer or strainer, a long-handled slotted spoon, a metal spatula or pancake turner, and various doughnut and biscuit cutters. Special doughnut cutters exist, which range from $2\frac{1}{2}$ to $3\frac{1}{2}$ inches in diameter, but a $2\frac{1}{2}$- to $3\frac{1}{2}$-inch biscuit cutter may also be used, with a smaller circular piece, such as a small cookie or aspic cutter, employed to cut the center hole, if needed. For Rosettes, the proper metal tool is essential.

COOKING METHODS AND TEMPERATURES

In many of the recipes, I have offered a choice between baking or frying the food. Where baking is suggested as an alternative, there is usually a difference in texture and taste, the baked version being slightly heavier and having, I feel, a less pronounced flavor. I prefer the few additional calories to the oven product, but again, this is a matter of taste. Furthermore, frying is the fastest technique of all.

Research experiments in which the amount of cooking oil is measured before and after frying reveal that only minute quantities of the oil have been absorbed by the food. This is because the surface of the food is quickly dehydrated by the high temperature of the oil and sealed. Therefore, the fat does not penetrate the interior. The temperature of the oil itself should stay between 340° and 380°F, which is the ideal range for frying. The temperature of the oil must not reach the smoking stage, or 450°F, because the oil then becomes saturated and should be discarded. All temperatures cited in the recipes are for sea level; for altitudes of 1,000 to 5,000 feet above sea level, the temperatures should be reduced by 5 to 10 percent.

The food must enter the hot oil by sliding from a utensil such as a spatula, and small amounts of food should be added at a time to avoid lowering the temperature of the oil too much. Keep an empty burner available when frying so that the pan can be lifted off the heat when the temperature gets too hot, particularly when using an electric stove. The oil should be allowed to regain the proper temperature between batches.

Doughnuts should be turned only once during the frying process, so check to see that the underside is properly browned before turning with a slotted spoon. Beignets, crullers, and some other foods may be turned frequently during frying to ensure even browning. The fried food should be lifted out with a slotted spoon, and any stray particles should be skimmed out of the oil after frying each batch. Drain the fried food on paper towels or absorbent paper, and then transfer to a rack to cool if indicated. If the doughnuts are to be dredged or shaken in a bag with a topping, they should still be warm.

Other foods for frying must be completely dry, or if dipped in a batter, any excess should be allowed to drip off into the bowl. If any water comes in contact with the hot oil, it will cause splattering. The pieces of food should be of uniform size and at room temperature.

STORING DOUGHNUTS

Doughnuts are without a doubt best eaten on the day they are made. However, any leftovers, fried or baked, may be stored for up to two days in an airtight container lined with wax paper. They may also be wrapped in freezer paper and frozen, the sooner after they are cooked the better. To defrost, unwrap the doughnuts and put them on a baking sheet in a preheated 300°F oven for a few minutes. I don't recommend refrigeration for either baked or fried foods.

YEAST DOUGHNUTS

OLD-FASHIONED YEAST DOUGHNUTS
About 12 pieces

∞

This is a basic sweet yeast dough, variations of which exist in almost every corner of the world. No matter what the ethnic source, though, one doughnut is never enough. You can double this recipe if you anticipate a hungry group!

1	package dry yeast or 1 heaping teaspoon bulk dry yeast
¼	cup warm water (105°F to 115°F)
¼	cup warm milk (105°F to 115°F)
¼	cup sugar
	Pinch of salt or to taste
1	large egg, lightly beaten
3	tablespoons vegetable oil
2 to 2½	cups unbleached flour, plus extra for rolling out and cutting
½	teaspoon ground nutmeg or mace
	Vegetable oil for frying
	Sugar for sprinkling

In a large bowl or the bowl of an electric mixer, sprinkle the yeast over the water. Stir to dissolve. Add the milk, sugar, salt, egg, and oil and beat in 1 cup of the flour until the mixture is smooth.

Sift 1 more cup of the flour with the nutmeg or mace in a small bowl, and beat it into the yeast mixture with a wooden spoon. Add enough of the remaining flour to make a soft, manageable dough. Cover and let rise in a warm, draft-free place until the dough is doubled in volume, about 1 hour.

Punch down the dough and turn out onto a well-floured surface. Turn the dough to cover it entirely with flour, adding flour as needed. Knead 8 or 10 times, or until elastic and smooth. Cover the dough with a large inverted bowl and let rest 15 minutes. Using a floured rolling pin, roll out the dough to a ½-inch thickness. Cut circles with a floured doughnut cutter and lift the doughnuts with a pancake turner to a floured cloth or surface. Reroll the scraps and cut additional doughnuts, keeping the holes to fry separately, if desired. Cover the doughnuts with a cloth and let double in size, about 45 minutes.

Meanwhile, in a deep pan bring at least 2 inches of oil to 375°F over moderate heat. With a spatula slide the doughnuts into the oil, cooking 2 or 3 at a time. When the undersides are golden brown, after about 1½ minutes, turn with a slotted spoon. Fry until golden brown on both sides, about 3 minutes in all. Drain on paper towels. While still warm, place the doughnuts on a rack over wax paper and sprinkle with sugar or shake the doughnuts with the sugar in a paper bag.

Variation: **CRULLERS**
Knead the dough as for doughnuts and let rest, covered with a bowl for 15 minutes. Roll out with a floured rolling pin to a 7 by 12-inch rectangle. With a sharp knife or pizza cutter, cut twelve 7-inch strips. Fold each strip in half, pinch the ends firmly together, and pull

gently to a 4-inch length. Twist twice and set aside on a floured cloth. Cover the twists with another cloth and let double in volume, about 45 minutes.

In a deep pan, bring at least 2 inches of oil to 375°F over moderate heat. With a spatula lower the crullers into the oil, cooking 2 at a time. Turn with a slotted spoon when golden brown, about 1½ minutes, and lift out when golden brown on both sides, about 3 minutes in all. Drain on paper towels. While warm, transfer the crullers to a rack over wax paper and sprinkle with sugar or shake the crullers with the sugar in a paper bag.

JELLY DOUGHNUTS
About 8 to 10 pieces

As any child can show you, it is necessary to hold a hand under your chin when taking the first bite of a jelly doughnut. Caution is needed or the luscious filling will all spurt out. These doughnuts are also called Bismarck or Berlin doughnuts, which reveals their probable origin. The jam or jelly should be a highly flavored one—like raspberry, plum, or apricot.

1 package dry yeast or 1 heaping teaspoon bulk dry yeast
¼ cup warm water (105°F to 115°F)
½ cup milk, warmed with 5 tablespoons unsalted butter or ¼ cup vegetable oil

Pinch of salt
1/2   cup sugar
1   large egg, lightly beaten
3 to 3 1/2   cups unbleached flour, plus extra for rolling out
       and cutting
1/2   teaspoon ground nutmeg or mace
3/4   cup jam or jelly of choice
       Vegetable oil for frying
1   cup sugar mixed with 1 teaspoon ground
       cinnamon

In a large bowl or the bowl of an electric mixer, sprinkle the yeast over the water and stir to dissolve. Stir in the milk mixture, salt, and sugar. Add the egg and mix well, then beat in 2 cups of the flour until smooth. Let the batter stand, covered, for 30 minutes. Sift in 1 cup of the remaining flour with the nutmeg or mace and stir into the batter with a wooden spoon.

Turn out the dough onto a well-floured surface and knead for 2 minutes with floured hands. Add more flour if needed so the dough isn't sticky. Place the dough in an oiled bowl and cover with plastic wrap or a towel. Let stand in a warm, draft-free place until doubled in volume, about 1 hour.

Roll the dough out on a floured surface with a floured rolling pin to a 1/4-inch thickness. With a biscuit cutter, cut rounds and gather the scraps together to roll again. On half of the rounds place 1 rounded teaspoon of jam or jelly. With a pastry brush, moisten the edges of the circles with water and cover with the remaining rounds. Pinch the edges to seal and cover with a cloth to let double again, about 1 hour.

In a deep pan, bring at least 2 inches of oil to 375°F over moderate heat. Lift the doughnuts with a pancake turner and slide them into the oil, cooking 2 at a time. They will rise to the surface. When golden brown on the underside, after about 2 minutes, turn with a slotted spoon. When the doughnuts are golden brown on both sides, about 5 minutes in all, lift out and drain on paper towels. Transfer to a rack over wax paper. While still warm, roll in the sugar mixture.

Variation: **CREAM BUNS**
Simply substitute cream filling for the jam or jelly.

CREAM FILLING

1½	cups milk
½	cup sugar
6	tablespoons unbleached flour
2	tablespoons cornstarch
3	large egg yolks, beaten
1	teaspoon almond extract

In a small, heavy saucepan, scald the milk. In a small bowl, combine the sugar, flour, and cornstarch. Mix well and whisk into the hot milk all at once. Cook over medium heat, stirring constantly, until it comes to a boil. Pour a small amount of the mixture over the egg yolks in a small bowl, then pour the mixture back into the saucepan. Cook over medium-low heat, stirring, until it boils and thickens. Remove from the heat and stir in the almond extract. Place a round of wax paper directly on the surface of the cream. When cool, refrigerate until ready to use, from 1 to 24 hours.

MARTHA WASHINGTON'S
CHERRY BALLS
About 12 pieces

∽

Happily for us, many colonial housewives kept journals and we have access to their "receipts" in the surviving ones, such as Mary Randolph's, Susannah Carter's, and the first First Lady's. Martha Washington used a hop yeast similar to the brewer's yeast we use today. The sugar was probably molasses and the cherries came from her orchard, possibly from the tree that later entered into American folklore.

1 package dry yeast or 1 heaping teaspoon bulk
   dry yeast
2 tablespoons sugar
½ cup warm milk (105°F to 115°F)
2 cups unbleached flour, plus extra for rolling out
   and cutting
   Pinch of salt
1½ tablespoons lard or unsalted margarine
1 large egg, well beaten
12 candied cherries
   Vegetable oil for frying
½ cup sugar mixed with 1 teaspoon ground
   cinnamon

Stir the yeast and ½ teaspoon of the sugar into the warm milk and set aside for 30 minutes. In a large bowl, mix the flour, salt, and the rest of the sugar. Cut in the lard or margarine until crumbly. Make a well in the flour mixture and stir in the milk mixture and the beaten egg. Cover tightly with plastic wrap and set aside in a warm, draft-free place until the dough is doubled in volume, about 1 hour.

Turn the dough out onto a floured surface and knead briefly. Form into a log-shaped roll and divide it into 12 equal pieces. Form each into a ball. With your finger, push a candied cherry into the middle of each ball and pinch the hole together. Place the balls on a floured surface, cover with a cloth, and let double in volume, about 45 minutes.

Fill a deep pan no more than halfway with oil, at least 2 inches, and bring it slowly to 375°F over moderate heat. With a slotted spoon lower the balls into the oil, cooking 3 or 4 at a time, and turn with the slotted spoon until golden brown on all sides, about 1½ minutes in all. Lift out the balls and drain them on paper towels. Roll the warm balls in the sugar mixture or shake them with the mixture in a paper bag.

SNAIL BUNS
About 18 pieces

∽

For *a football-watching afternoon, these buns,
also known as Schnecken, are as wonderful as they come,
hot from the kitchen accompanied by cider or whatever.
The raisins or nuts can be omitted to save time, and if
they fall out during the frying, scoop them up with a
slotted spoon before the next batch of buns is cooked.*

¾	cup milk
1	cup sugar
¼	cup (½ stick) unsalted butter
1	package dry yeast or 1 heaping teaspoon bulk dry yeast
¼	cup warm water (105°F to 115°F)
1	large egg, lightly beaten
3 to 3 ½	cups unbleached flour
3	tablespoons water
1	teaspoon ground cinnamon
½	cup raisins or chopped nuts (optional)
	Vegetable oil for frying or baking

In a small, heavy saucepan scald the milk, then
remove the pan from the heat and stir in ¼ cup of the
sugar and the butter. Cool the mixture to lukewarm.

Sprinkle the yeast over the ¼ cup of warm water in
a large bowl and stir to dissolve. Add the milk mixture
and the egg to the bowl and stir to combine. Whisk in
1½ cups of the flour. Cover with a towel and set aside for

45 minutes in a warm, draft-free place. Beat in more flour until a firm dough is formed. Cover again and let rise until doubled in volume, about 1 hour, in a warm, draft-free place.

Meanwhile, mix the remaining ¾ cup of sugar and 3 tablespoons of water in a small, heavy saucepan over moderate heat and stir until the sugar dissolves. Bring to a boil and let boil 1 minute, then remove from the heat. Cool the syrup, then add the cinnamon and set aside until needed.

Punch down the dough and turn it out onto a floured surface. Knead briefly and divide it into halves. Roll out one half to a 14 by 9-inch rectangle. Brush with half the syrup and sprinkle the raisins or nuts on evenly, if desired. Roll up from the short side tightly and seal the seam by brushing the edge of the dough lightly with water and pressing together gently. Cut into 9 equal pieces. Repeat with the remaining half of the dough. Place the pieces on a greased baking sheet, cut sides up. Press lightly to flatten and cover with a towel. Let double in size, about 30 to 40 minutes.

To fry the buns, fill a deep pan no more than halfway with oil, at least 2 inches, and bring it slowly to 375°F over moderate heat. Dip a pancake turner in the hot oil and slide the buns into the oil. Cook 2 or 3 at a time until golden brown on each side, about 3 minutes in all. Lift out with a slotted spoon and let any excess oil drip back into the pan. Drain on paper towels and serve warm.

To bake the buns, preheat the oven to 375°F. Line a baking sheet with parchment paper and place the buns 1 inch apart on it. Brush each lightly with oil. Bake 25 to 30 minutes, or until golden brown. Serve warm.

RICE DOUGHNUTS (CALAS)
About 10 to 12 pieces

∞

In New Orleans many years ago, Creole women walked the streets in the early morning crying their wares: these golden balls of rice called Calas. The yeast and rice batter rises during the night and is ready in less than an hour for breakfast.

2	cups water
⅔	cup long-grain rice
2	packages dry yeast or 2 heaping teaspoons bulk dry yeast
¼	cup granulated sugar
3	large eggs
1½	cups unbleached flour
1	teaspoon ground cinnamon
1	teaspoon ground nutmeg
	Pinch of salt
	Vegetable oil for frying
	Confectioners' sugar (optional)

Bring the water to a boil and add the rice. Stir once or twice to distribute the grains, then lower the heat. Cover and let simmer over medium-low heat for 15 minutes. Remove from the heat and cool until tepid, then add the yeast. Mix well and cover tightly with plastic wrap. Refrigerate overnight. Allow the mixture to stand before continuing.

Whisk the sugar and eggs together and stir into the yeast mixture. Combine the flour with the cinnamon, nutmeg, and salt and add to the yeast mixture by half cupfuls, stirring well each time. With wet hands, form 2-inch balls about the size of a golf ball.

Fill a deep pan no more than halfway with oil, at least 2 inches, and bring the oil slowly to 350°F over moderate heat. With a slotted spoon slide the balls into the oil, cooking 3 or 4 at a time. Turn with a slotted spoon until golden brown all over, about 2 minutes in all. Lift out the doughnuts and drain on paper towels. Serve immediately with confectioners' sugar on the side, if desired.

POTATO DOUGHNUTS
About 18 pieces

∾

Mashed potatoes formed a much greater part of our forerunners' diet than they do today, despite the efforts of modern nutritionists to convince the calorie-conscious public that they are not just starch. These doughnuts are so delicious that it is worth boiling two baking potatoes and mashing them just for this purpose.

    2   packages dry yeast or 2 heaping teaspoons bulk
        dry yeast
    ½   cup warm water (105°F to 115°F)
    2   cups milk
    ½   cup sugar
    ½   cup vegetable oil
        Pinch of salt
    3   large eggs, lightly beaten
    1   cup mashed potatoes
3 to 3½ cups unbleached flour
        Vegetable oil for frying
    1   cup sugar
    2   tablespoons grated lemon peel

In a large bowl, sprinkle the yeast over the water and stir to dissolve. Scald the milk in a heavy saucepan, then remove from the heat and stir in the sugar, oil, and salt. Cool, then add this to the yeast mixture.

In a medium bowl, blend the eggs into the potatoes until smooth. Whisk this into the milk mixture, then

24

slowly add the flour, 1 cup at a time, beating thoroughly by hand or by mixer. When it becomes a smooth dough, add additional flour slowly, mixing with a wooden spoon until the dough is thick enough to support the spoon upright, but not too stiff. Cover the bowl tightly with plastic wrap and let double in a warm, draft-free place, about 1 hour. Alternately, the dough can be refrigerated, where it will rise overnight.

Punch the dough down and turn out onto a well-floured surface. Cover with a towel and let rest until doubled again, about 1 hour. It will take about 1½ hours if it has been refrigerated.

Divide the dough in half, and roll one half out to a ½-inch thickness. With a floured doughnut cutter, cut out rings. Repeat with the remaining dough, either incorporating the holes or keeping them to fry separately. Continue rerolling and cutting until all the dough is used up.

Fill a deep pan no more than halfway with oil, at least 2 inches, and bring to 375°F over moderate heat. Slide each doughnut in the oil with a metal spatula, cooking 2 or 3 at a time. Turn with a slotted spoon after about 1½ minutes, cooking until golden brown on both sides, about 3 minutes in all. Remove with a slotted spoon, allowing the excess oil to drain back into the pan, then drain the doughnuts on paper towels. In a paper bag, mix the sugar and lemon peel. While still warm, shake each doughnut in the bag and set on racks until ready to serve.

ONION BUNS
About 18 pieces

∽

Just the fragrance of these buns—either fried or baked—will alert a whole houseful of sleepers. Accompanied by crisp bacon and fried apples, they are fortifying as well as morale boosting. Forget the cholesterol for one morning!

1	package dry yeast or 1 heaping teaspoon bulk dry yeast
1/4	cup warm water (105°F to 115°F)
1	large onion, minced
3	tablespoons unsalted butter or margarine
3/4	cup milk
1	teaspoon honey
1/2	teaspoon freshly ground pepper
1/2	teaspoon celery salt
2¾	cups unbleached flour, plus extra as needed
	Vegetable oil for frying or baking

In a small bowl, stir the yeast into the water until dissolved. In a heavy, medium-sized saucepan, sauté the onion in 1 tablespoon of the butter until soft and transparent, but not brown, about 4 minutes. Add the milk and the rest of the butter. Heat the mixture to just warm (115°F) over moderate heat and add the honey.

In a large bowl, combine the pepper, celery salt, and flour. Make a well in the center and stir in the yeast and the milk mixture. Add flour if needed to make a firm dough. Mix thoroughly, then turn out onto a floured surface and knead for 5 minutes. Cover with the bowl and let double in volume, about 1½ hours.

Punch down the dough and pinch off 2-inch pieces. On a lightly floured surface, pat or roll each piece into a 3-inch circle. Repeat with all of the dough, cover the rounds with a cloth, and let rise for 45 minutes.

To fry the buns, fill a deep pan no more than halfway with oil, at least 2 inches, and slowly bring it to 375°F over moderate heat. Slide the rounds into the oil with a pancake turner, cooking 2 or 3 at a time. Turn the buns with a slotted spoon when golden brown on the underside and cook until golden brown on both sides, about 3 minutes in all. Lift out with a slotted spoon and drain on paper towels. Transfer to a wire rack.

To bake the buns, preheat the oven to 375°F. Place the rounds, 2 inches apart, on a greased baking sheet and brush each bun lightly with oil. Bake for 25 minutes, or until golden brown. Cool on a rack.

LITTLE RINGS
About 12 to 15 pieces

∽

When dinner-table conversation in Paris comes to a sudden lull, it is simple to revive it by asking innocently, "What is the difference between a bugne *and a* bugnon *?" Every province in France has a cherished type of fried dough, and discussion can become very heated over the relative merits of each, and even more over how to make them. The name simply depends on the origin of the fried dough. This particular* bugnon *is native to Bercy, the area around Paris.*

4   tablespoons warm milk (105°F to 115°F)
1   tablespoon granulated sugar
2   tablespoons walnut oil
1   package dry yeast or 1 heaping teaspoon bulk
      dry yeast
1½ cups unbleached flour, plus extra for forming
¼   cup finely ground walnuts
      Vegetable oil for frying
      Confectioners' sugar

In a medium bowl, mix the milk, sugar, and oil, then stir in the yeast until dissolved. Beat in the flour and walnuts. Mix thoroughly and cover tightly with plastic wrap. Set aside in a warm, draft-free place until doubled, about 1 hour.

Punch down the dough and turn out onto a floured surface. Pinch off pieces the size of a walnut and roll each into a narrow rope about 3 inches long. Join the ends and pinch together to form a small ring. Repeat with all the dough and cover the rings with a towel. Let them rise until doubled, about 30 minutes.

Fill a deep pan no more than halfway with oil, at least 2 inches, and slowly bring it to 375°F over moderate heat. Lower the rings into the oil with a pancake turner, cooking 2 or 3 rings at a time. When golden brown on the underside, after about 1½ minutes, turn the rings with a slotted spoon. When both sides are golden brown, about 3 minutes in all, lift out with a slotted spoon and drain on paper towels. Cool on a rack over wax paper and sprinkle with confectioners' sugar.

Buns with Fruit Purees
About 16 pieces

∽

Originally these sweet treats were filled with golden greengage plum jam, not the too-common purple ones that flood our markets in high summer. I fancy filling them with a freshly made puree of yellow plums, or nectarines, or even pears.

2 packages dry yeast or 2 heaping teaspoons bulk dry yeast
1/2 cup warm water (105°F to 115°F)
3 cups unbleached flour, plus extra for rolling out and cutting
5 tablespoons granulated sugar
2/3 cup milk at room temperature
1/4 cup (1/2 stick) unsalted butter, melted
3 large eggs, well beaten
   Vegetable oil for frying
   Confectioners' sugar

FRUIT PUREE

1 pound fruit of choice (such as plums, nectarines, pears), sliced
1/2 cup water
1 cup granulated sugar or to taste
   Ground cinnamon, cloves, nutmeg, or vanilla extract to taste (optional)

In a large bowl, stir the yeast into the water until dissolved. Mix the flour and sugar in another large bowl.

Make a well and pour in the yeast mixture, milk, and melted butter. Beat well and add the eggs. Mix thoroughly and cover tightly with plastic wrap. Set aside in a warm, draft-free place and let double, 1 to 1½ hours.

Meanwhile, make the Fruit Puree. Peel the fruit, except for plums, and core or remove pits. In a small, heavy saucepan, mix the water and sugar and stir over moderate heat until the sugar is dissolved. Raise the heat to medium-high, bring the mixture to a boil, and cook for 2 minutes; remove from the heat and cool. Add the fruit to the syrup and bring to a simmer over low heat. Cook 5 or 10 minutes, or until soft. Pass the fruit through a food mill or whirl in a food processor. Cinnamon, cloves, nutmeg, or vanilla may be added.

Punch down the dough and turn out onto a floured surface. Divide it in half and form each half into a roll. Cut each roll into 8 equal pieces. With a floured rolling pin, roll each piece into a 3-inch round. Brush the edges with water and place the round in the palm of your hand. Place a rounded teaspoonful of puree in the center and bring the edges together, pinching them to seal. Place the buns, seam side down, on a lightly floured cloth 2 inches apart. Cover with another towel and let double, about 1 hour.

Fill a deep pan no more than halfway with oil, at least 2 inches, and bring it slowly to 375°F over moderate heat. Dip a pancake turner into the hot oil and slide the buns into the oil, cooking 2 or 3 at a time. Turn with a slotted spoon when the underside is golden brown, after about 2 minutes. Lift out with a slotted spoon when both sides are golden brown, about 4 minutes in all. Drain on paper towels and transfer to a rack over wax paper. Dust with confectioners' sugar.

BAKING POWDER AND SODA DOUGHNUTS

CHOCOLATE–CHOCOLATE CHIP DOUGHNUTS

About 12 pieces

∽

It is mandatory to have something chocolate in every cookbook, and if possible, to combine several different kinds of chocolate. I entertained the neighborhood's youth several times while trying out recipes, which culminated in this one, pronounced super by all.

To exaggerate the chocolateness even further, a glaze can be added to the finished doughnut. The frying oil becomes dark immediately on the addition of the first few doughnuts and should be discarded at the end of the cooking process, or you can filter it and keep it for the next batch of chocolate doughnuts.

1¾	cups unbleached flour, plus extra for rolling out and cutting
1	teaspoon baking powder
½	teaspoon baking soda
½	cup granulated sugar
½	cup buttermilk
1½	tablespoons vegetable oil
1	large egg
3	tablespoons unsweetened cocoa
1	cup chocolate chips, coarsely chopped, or mini chocolate chips
	Vegetable oil for frying or baking

    2   1-ounce squares unsweetened chocolate
    4   tablespoons (½ stick) unsalted butter or
          margarine
    2   cups confectioners' sugar
    4   tablespoons boiling water

Into a large bowl or the bowl of a mixer, sift the flour, baking powder, baking soda, and sugar together. In a small bowl, whisk the buttermilk and oil together with the egg. Stir the cocoa into the flour mixture and add the egg mixture. Mix thoroughly and turn out onto a floured surface. Knead in the chocolate chips and flatten the dough slightly into a round. Wrap in wax paper or plastic wrap and refrigerate for at least 1 hour.

Meanwhile, make the Chocolate Glaze, if desired. Melt the chocolate and butter in a double boiler over medium heat. Beat in the confectioners' sugar, then stir in the water. Remove from the heat and place a round of wax paper directly on the surface of the glaze. If the glaze hardens, warm over hot water before applying to the doughnuts.

Divide the dough in half, returning half to the refrigerator, and roll out half to a ½-inch thickness on a lightly floured surface. Cut out doughnuts with a doughnut cutter. Set the doughnuts aside and cut additional doughnuts with the other half of the dough. Incorporate the scraps and doughnut holes and cut doughnuts until the dough is used up. Cover the doughnuts with a cloth until ready to cook.

To fry the doughnuts, fill a deep pan no more than halfway with oil, at least 2 inches, and bring it slowly to

375°F over moderate heat. Slide the doughnuts into the oil with a pancake turner, cooking 2 or 3 at a time. Turn with a slotted spoon after 1 minute. Since the doughnuts are dark in color and the color of the crust cannot be determined, timing is crucial. Cook for 1 more minute and lift out with a slotted spoon to drain on paper towels. Cool on a rack and dip in Chocolate Glaze, if desired.

To bake the doughnuts, preheat the oven to 400°F. Oil a baking sheet and place doughnuts 1 inch apart. Brush the doughnuts lightly with oil and bake 18 to 22 minutes, or until a toothpick inserted in a doughnut comes out clean. Cool on a rack and dip in Chocolate Glaze, if desired.

BAKING POWDER DOUGHNUTS
AND CRULLERS
About 18 to 20 pieces

∞

This is another basic recipe, probably close to the one used in Adolph Levitt's machine, to say nothing of Dunkin' Donuts or Mr. Doughnut. The doughnuts can be successfully baked, but I don't recommend baking the Crullers, which become quite heavy.

    3 large eggs
    1 cup sugar
    2 tablespoons (¼ stick) unsalted butter or
           margarine, softened
    4 cups unbleached flour, plus extra for rolling out
           and cutting
    1 tablespoon baking powder
       Pinch of salt
    ¾ teaspoon ground nutmeg
    ¾ cup milk
       Vegetable oil for frying
    1 cup sugar mixed with 1 teaspoon ground
           cinnamon

In a large bowl, whisk together the eggs, sugar, and butter. In another bowl, sift the flour with the baking powder, salt, and nutmeg. Add half the flour mixture to the egg mixture, beating with a wooden spoon. Beat in the milk, then beat in the rest of the flour mixture until a soft dough is formed.

Cover the bowl with plastic wrap and refrigerate for 1 hour. Remove half the dough, refrigerating the other half, to a well-floured cloth and turn to coat with flour.

To make doughnuts, roll the dough on a lightly floured surface with a floured rolling pin to a $\frac{1}{2}$-inch thickness. Cut doughnuts with a floured doughnut cutter. With a pancake turner, lift the doughnuts to a floured surface. Roll out the remaining dough and cut additional doughnuts until all the dough has been used. Cover all with a cloth and let rest 15 minutes.

To make Crullers, roll out the dough to a $\frac{1}{4}$-inch thickness and with a floured pizza cutter or sharp knife, cut in strips 1 inch wide and 6 inches long. Double each strip lengthwise in 2. Pinch the ends together and twist. Repeat with all the strips, transfer them to a floured surface, cover with a towel, and let rest for 15 minutes.

Meanwhile, fill a deep pan no more than halfway with oil, at least 2 inches, and bring it slowly to 375°F over moderate heat. With a pancake turner, slide each doughnut or cruller into the oil, cooking 2 or 3 at a time. Turn the doughnuts or crullers with a slotted spoon when golden brown on the underside, about $1\frac{1}{2}$ minutes. When both sides are golden brown, about 3 minutes in all, lift out with a slotted spoon to drain on paper towels, letting any excess oil drip back into the pan. Shake the doughnuts in a paper bag with the sugar and cinnamon or frost with the Orange Glaze or Vanilla Cream Frosting (pages 46 and 50).

To bake the doughnuts, preheat the oven to 375°F. Place them 2 inches apart on a greased baking sheet and bake the doughnuts until golden brown, about 20 minutes. Remove to a rack over wax paper and sprinkle with the sugar and cinnamon or frost as directed above.

SWEET POTATO DOUGHNUTS

About 2 dozen pieces

❧

A modest American genius, George Washington Carver appeared before Congress at the time of the grave wheat shortage during World War I and demonstrated how bread could be made with sweet potatoes. He claimed that two major subjects of his research, peanuts and sweet potatoes, alone furnished enough nutritious and varied food for an entire day's diet. Valid or not, these doughnuts are pure pleasure.

2	large eggs, well beaten
3/4	cup sugar
3	tablespoons unsalted butter or margarine, melted
3/4	cup mashed sweet potatoes (1 large boiled sweet potato)
3 1/2	cups unbleached flour
4	teaspoons baking powder
1/4	teaspoon ground cinnamon
1/4	teaspoon ground nutmeg
4	tablespoons milk
	Vegetable oil for frying or baking
1	cup sugar mixed with 1 teaspoon ground cinnamon

In a large bowl, whisk together the eggs, sugar, and butter. Stir in the mashed sweet potatoes and blend well. In another bowl, sift together the flour, baking powder, cinnamon, and nutmeg. Stir the flour mixture by thirds into the potato mixture, alternating with halves of the milk, ending with the flour mixture. Cover the bowl with plastic wrap and refrigerate for at least 1 hour.

Divide the dough in half and keep half refrigerated while rolling out the other half on a floured surface to a ½-inch thickness. Cut out doughnuts with a doughnut cutter, transferring the doughnuts and their separate holes to a baking sheet lined with parchment paper. Cover with a towel and refrigerate while rolling and cutting the second half of the dough.

To fry the doughnuts, fill a deep pan no more than halfway with oil, at least 2 inches, and slowly bring the oil to 375°F over moderate heat. Slide the doughnuts into the oil with a pancake turner, cooking 2 or 3 at a time. Turn with a slotted spoon when the underside is golden brown. When both sides are golden brown, about 3 minutes in all, lift out with a slotted spoon and drain on paper towels. Transfer to a rack over wax paper and sprinkle with the sugar mixture.

To bake the doughnuts, preheat the oven to 375°F. Place the chilled doughnuts with their separate holes on a greased baking sheet at least 1 inch apart, and brush the doughnuts and holes with oil. Bake until golden brown, about 15 minutes. Spread the sugar mixture on wax paper. Brush the warm doughnuts lightly with oil and roll in the sugar mixture.

SOUR CREAM DOUGHNUTS
About 2 dozen pieces

∽

Sour cream makes these doughnuts very light. Stirred together in the evening, the dough can be refrigerated overnight and used in the morning in time for breakfast.

3 large eggs
1 cup granulated sugar
1 cup sour cream
1 teaspoon baking soda
3¼ cups unbleached flour, plus extra for rolling out and cutting
1 teaspoon ground nutmeg
Pinch of salt (optional)
Vegetable oil for frying or baking
Confectioners' sugar (optional)

Whisk together the eggs and sugar in a large bowl. In another bowl, mix the sour cream with the baking soda and stir into the egg mixture. In a small bowl, sift together the flour, nutmeg, and salt, if desired. Gradually stir the flour mixture into the sour cream mixture. Mix thoroughly and cover with plastic wrap. Refrigerate at least 3 hours or overnight.

Let the dough return to room temperature and turn out onto a floured surface. Roll out the dough to a ½-inch thickness. Cut out rings with a doughnut cutter. Place the doughnuts with their holes on a floured towel and cover with another towel. Let rest for 15 minutes.

To fry the doughnuts, fill a deep pan no more than halfway with oil, at least 2 inches, and bring it slowly to 375°F over moderate heat. Slide the doughnuts into the oil with a pancake turner, cooking 2 or 3 at a time. Turn with a slotted spoon when golden brown on the underside, after about 1½ minutes, and lift out with a slotted spoon when both sides are golden brown, about 3 minutes in all. Drain on paper towels and transfer to a rack over wax paper. Sprinkle with confectioners' sugar, if desired.

To bake the doughnuts, preheat the oven to 375°F. Place the doughnuts with their holes 1 inch apart on an oiled baking sheet and brush with oil. Bake the doughnuts for 20 to 30 minutes, or until golden brown. Remove to a rack over wax paper and sprinkle with confectioners' sugar, if desired.

FRYING PAN COOKIES

About 3 dozen pieces

∞

Grandmothers who must compete with fast-food doughnut shops whose attractive products are made from chemical-laden mixes will find these little impromptu cakes a welcome boon. Whether baked or fried, this recipe is equally fast and popular, and it is comforting to know that there are no preservatives! The recipe may be doubled or tripled.

1	cup (2 sticks) unsalted butter or margarine
1/4	cup granulated sugar
1	large egg, lightly beaten
1	cup unbleached flour, plus extra for rolling out and shaping
1	teaspoon baking powder
1	teaspoon ground cinnamon or nutmeg
	Vegetable oil for frying or baking

FROSTING (OPTIONAL)

1	egg white, lightly beaten
1	cup confectioners' sugar
1/4	teaspoon vanilla, lemon, or almond extract

Cream together the butter and sugar in a large bowl. Whisk in the egg. In a small bowl, sift together the flour, baking powder, and cinnamon or nutmeg. Mix the flour mixture thoroughly into the butter mixture and form into a ball. Wrap the dough in wax paper and chill for at least 30 minutes, or up to 3 days.

Divide the dough and refrigerate half until needed. Roll out half on a floured surface to a $1/16$-inch thickness, and cut out 2-inch rounds with a cookie or biscuit cutter.

To fry the cookies, generously oil a heavy skillet or griddle and place over moderate heat until a drop of water skates over the surface. Lift the cakes with a pancake turner and cook 4 or 5 at a time. They will begin to puff almost immediately. When the underside is brown, about 1 minute, turn and brown the other side for up to a minute. Lift out and set on a rack.

To bake the cookies, preheat the oven to 375°F and lightly brush a baking sheet with oil. Bake for 3 minutes, or until the underside of the cookies is brown. Turn them with a pancake turner and bake 1 minute longer, or until golden brown. Lift off the baking sheet and cool on a wire rack.

To make the frosting, mix the egg white, confectioners' sugar, and desired flavoring. Spread the frosting on the cookies after they have cooled with a small spatula or brush.

APPLE DOUGHNUTS
About 18 pieces

∽

What would Halloween be without doughnuts and cider? And what could be better than doughnuts flavored with apples and cider? Use Golden Delicious apples or any other sweet eating apple if you decide to make the sauce yourself.

$1/2$	cup brown sugar, firmly packed
$1/4$	cup vegetable oil
$1/4$	cup buttermilk
$1/4$	cup apple cider or apple juice
1	large egg
1	cup unsweetened applesauce
$2^1/2$ to 3	cups unbleached flour, plus extra for rolling out and cutting
1	teaspoon ground mace
1	teaspoon ground cinnamon
1	teaspoon baking powder
$1/2$	teaspoon baking soda
	Vegetable oil for frying or baking
	Confectioners' sugar (optional)

In a large bowl, combine the brown sugar, oil, buttermilk, and cider. Whisk in the egg and applesauce. In a small bowl, sift together $2^1/2$ cups of the flour, mace, cinnamon, baking powder, and baking soda. Add the flour mixture to the cider mixture and mix to make a soft dough, adding flour if needed. Turn the dough out onto

44

a floured surface and with floured hands knead gently until the dough is smooth and no longer sticky.

Roll the dough out to a ½-inch thickness and cut out rounds with a floured doughnut cutter. Place them with their holes on a baking sheet lined with parchment paper and refrigerate, covered, until ready to cook.

To fry the doughnuts, fill a deep pan no more than halfway with oil, at least 2 inches, and slowly bring it to 375°F over moderate heat. Dip a pancake turner in the hot oil and slide each doughnut into the oil, cooking 3 or 4 at a time. When golden brown on the underside, after about 1½ minutes, turn with a slotted spoon. When golden brown on both sides, about 3 minutes in all, lift out with a slotted spoon and drain on paper towels. Transfer to a rack over wax paper and sprinkle with confectioners' sugar, if desired.

To bake the doughnuts, place them 2 inches apart on a parchment paper–lined baking sheet and refrigerate, covered, until very firm, about 1 hour. Preheat the oven to 375°F. Brush the doughnuts with oil and bake until golden brown, about 20 minutes. Place them on a rack over wax paper and sprinkle with confectioners' sugar, if desired.

ORANGE PUFFS
About 3 dozen pieces

∽

These little bites are so full of sunshine that they can brighten any rainy day at breakfast or teatime. With or without the Orange Glaze, they lend a hint of my favorite Seville bittersweet marmalade to accompany your cup of Earl Grey or Lapsang Soochong.

1 navel orange
½ cup sour cream
¼ cup light brown sugar, firmly packed
¼ cup vegetable oil
1 large egg, lightly beaten
2 cups unbleached flour
2 teaspoons baking powder
½ teaspoon baking soda
   Pinch of salt
1 tablespoon orange juice
   Vegetable oil for frying

ORANGE GLAZE (OPTIONAL)

1½ cups confectioners' sugar
3 tablespoons orange juice
1 tablespoon grated orange zest

Grate the zest from the orange into a large bowl. Peel the remaining skin from the orange and cut the orange into sections. Remove any pits and pulse the orange in a food processor until finely minced but not pureed, or mince by hand. Add the pulp to the grated zest. Whisk in the sour cream, brown sugar, oil, and egg. In a small bowl, sift together the flour, baking powder, baking soda, and salt. Stir the flour mixture and the orange juice into the sour cream mixture and mix thoroughly. Refrigerate the batter, covered with plastic wrap, until ready to use, at least 1 hour and up to 24 hours.

Fill a deep pan with oil no more than halfway, at least 2 inches, and bring it slowly to 375°F over moderate heat. Dip a teaspoon in the hot oil and drop the batter by teaspoonfuls into the oil, redipping the spoon in the oil each time. Use another teaspoon to slide the batter off, cooking 5 or 6 puffs at a time. Turn the puffs with a slotted spoon until golden brown on all sides, about 2 minutes in all. Lift the puffs out with a slotted spoon and drain on paper towels. Transfer to a rack over wax paper.

To make the glaze, stir the confectioners' sugar, orange juice, and zest together in a small bowl. When the puffs are cool, dip them into the glaze and place on a rack until dry.

WHOLE WHEAT AND HONEY DOUGHNUTS
About 2 dozen pieces

You can point out to your health-conscious friends that these doughnuts are made with whole wheat flour, honey, yogurt, and no butter. Calories are their only worry.

2	large eggs
¾	cup dark brown sugar, firmly packed
¼	cup honey
½	cup plain yogurt
¼	cup vegetable oil
1	cup whole wheat flour
1½ to 2	cups unbleached flour
2	teaspoons baking powder
1	teaspoon baking soda
¼	teaspoon ground cardamom
½	teaspoon ground cinnamon
¼	teaspoon ground ginger
¼	teaspoon ground cloves
	Pinch of salt
	Vegetable oil for frying or baking
1	cup granulated sugar mixed with 1 teaspoon ground cinnamon for sprinkling

In a large bowl, whisk the eggs until foamy. Stir in the brown sugar, honey, yogurt, and oil. In another bowl, sift the whole wheat flour and 1½ cups of the unbleached flour together with the baking powder, baking soda, cardamom, cinnamon, ginger, and cloves. Sift this mixture over the egg mixture 1 cup at a time until a soft dough is formed, adding additional unbleached flour if needed. Cover the bowl tightly with plastic wrap and refrigerate for at least an hour or overnight.

Roll out the dough on a well-floured surface to a ½-inch thickness. Cut doughnuts with a floured doughnut cutter. Set aside on a floured surface and cover with a cloth until all are cut.

Fill a deep pan no more than halfway with oil, at least 2 inches, and bring it slowly to 375°F over moderate heat. Lift the doughnuts with a pancake turner and slide them into the oil, cooking 2 or 3 at a time. Turn with a slotted spoon when the underside is golden brown, cooking about 1 minute on each side. Lift out with a slotted spoon and drain on paper towels. Transfer to a rack over wax paper and sprinkle with the sugar mixture.

To bake the doughnuts, preheat the oven to 375°F and place the doughnuts on a well-oiled baking sheet 1 inch apart and brush with oil. Bake for 15 minutes, or until lightly browned. Cool on a rack over wax paper, then brush again with oil. Sprinkle with the sugar mixture.

COCONUT CAKE DOUGHNUTS
About 12 to 15 pieces

∽

The name says it all. For every birthday in the family, my mother made a special coconut cake straight out of the Joy of Cooking. From the coconut being cracked by a hammer on the back steps to the coconut "milk" jealously divided among us, to the final counting of the candles on top, it was an occasion. The icing for these doughnuts is optional but is an historical imperative for me.

2½ cups unbleached flour
2 teaspoons baking powder
Pinch of salt
¾ cup unsweetened flaked coconut
2 large eggs
½ cup granulated sugar
¼ cup milk
2 tablespoons vegetable oil
Vegetable oil for frying or baking

VANILLA CREAM FROSTING (OPTIONAL)

2 tablespoons unsalted butter or margarine, softened
1½ cups sifted confectioners' sugar
1 tablespoon light cream
½ teaspoon vanilla extract
½ cup unsweetened flaked coconut

In a large bowl, sift together the flour, baking powder, and salt. Stir in the coconut. In another bowl, beat the eggs and sugar until light. Beat in the milk and oil. Make a well in the flour mixture and beat in the egg mixture. Mix thoroughly and cover tightly with plastic wrap. Refrigerate for several hours or overnight.

Turn the dough out onto a floured surface and roll to a ½-inch thickness. Cut circles with a doughnut cutter. Incorporate the holes into the scraps, rerolling and cutting until the dough is used up. Set the doughnuts aside covered with a cloth until ready to cook.

Fill a deep pan no more than halfway with oil, at least 2 inches, and slowly bring it to 375°F over moderate heat. Slide the doughnuts into the oil with a pancake turner, cooking 2 or 3 at a time. Turn the doughnuts with a slotted spoon when the underside is golden brown, about 1½ minutes. When both sides are golden brown, about 3 minutes in all, lift out with a slotted spoon. Drain on paper towels and transfer to a rack over wax paper. When cool, ice with the frosting, if desired.

To bake the doughnuts, preheat the oven to 375°F. Place the doughnuts on an oiled baking sheet 1 inch apart. Brush with oil and refrigerate for 30 minutes. Bake for 20 minutes, or until golden brown. Remove to a rack over wax paper.

To make the frosting, cream together the butter and confectioners' sugar. Stir in the cream and vanilla, then mix in the coconut thoroughly. Spread on the cool doughnuts.

BRAIDS IN SYRUP
About 12 pieces

This dough is simple and very easy to handle. Soaking the Braids in Syrup is traditional in countries with a sweet tooth like those of the Middle East, but this syrup is much lighter than the customary honey-based syrup.

2   cups unbleached flour
1½ teaspoons baking powder
    Pinch of salt
2   tablespoons (¼ stick) unsalted butter, chilled
      and cut in pieces
1   large egg
3   tablespoons water
    Vegetable oil for frying

SYRUP

2½ cups sugar
1¼ cups water
1   tablespoon lemon juice
1   tablespoon rose water, orange blossom water, or
      vanilla extract

Sift the flour, baking powder, and salt together into a medium-sized bowl. Cut the butter into the flour mixture until it resembles cornmeal. Beat the egg and water together and stir into the flour mixture until it forms a ball. Cover the bowl with plastic wrap and refrigerate for 3 hours.

Meanwhile, start the Syrup. In a small, heavy saucepan, bring the sugar, water, and lemon juice to a boil over medium heat, then lower the heat and simmer for 5 or 10 minutes until it thickens. Set aside and cool. Stir in the rose water.

Turn out the dough on a floured surface and roll the dough to $1/16$-inch thickness. With a sharp knife or pizza cutter, cut into strips $3/4$-inch wide and 3 inches long. Cut each strip in 3 equal strips lengthwise and braid. Set aside on a floured towel and cover with another towel until ready to cook.

Fill a deep pan no more than halfway with oil, at least 2 inches, and bring it slowly to 375°F over moderate heat. Slide the braids with a pancake turner into the oil, cooking 2 or 3 at a time. Turn the braids with a slotted spoon when golden brown on the underside, after about $1\frac{1}{2}$ minutes, and lift out with a slotted spoon when both sides are golden brown, about 3 minutes in all. Drain the braids on paper towels. Meanwhile, gently reheat the syrup over low heat. Soak the braids in the warm syrup for 15 to 20 minutes. Drain on a rack over paper towels and serve.

ALMOND TURNOVERS
About 28 pieces

∽

Appropriate at teatime or with a glass of wine, these small empanaditas are a welcome variation on what the late James Beard called the cocktail hour's "dibs and dabs." Instead of the almond filling, they can be filled with anything you fancy: preserves, Fruit Puree (page 30), or even peanut butter.

    2   cups unbleached flour
    2   teaspoons baking powder
    ½   cup (1 stick) unsalted butter or lard
    ½   cup ice water, plus more as needed
        Vegetable oil for frying
    1   egg beaten with 1 tablespoon water

ALMOND FILLING
    ¾   cup finely chopped blanched almonds
    ½   cup sugar
    1   teaspoon ground cinnamon
    1   large egg white
    ¼   teaspoon almond extract

In a medium-sized bowl or the bowl of a food processor, combine the flour and baking powder. Cut in the butter or lard with your fingers, 2 knives, or the food processor and mix in the ½ cup of ice water, adding additional water as needed to make a firm dough. Wrap the dough in plastic wrap or wax paper and refrigerate at least 1 hour.

Meanwhile, make the filling. In a small bowl, mix the almonds, sugar, and cinnamon. In another small bowl, whisk the egg white until frothy but not stiff. Stir into the almond mixture, add the almond extract, and mix thoroughly. Set aside, covered with plastic wrap.

On a lightly floured surface, roll out the dough to a ⅛-inch thickness. Cut out rounds with a biscuit or cookie cutter. Place 1 teaspoon of filling on half of each round, moisten the edges with water, and fold half over to form a half moon. Press the edges with a fork to seal and set aside on a floured surface.

To fry the turnovers, fill a deep pan no more than halfway with oil, at least 2 inches, and bring it slowly to 375°F over moderate heat. Slide the turnovers into the oil with a pancake turner, cooking 3 or 4 at a time. Turn with a slotted spoon after 1 minute and lift out when golden brown on both sides, about 2 minutes in all. Drain on paper towels.

To bake the turnovers, arrange them 1 inch apart on an oiled baking sheet and chill for 30 minutes, covered with a cloth. Preheat the oven to 375°F. Brush the turnovers with the egg mixture and bake for 20 minutes, or until golden brown. Cool on a rack.

TEATIME DAINTIES
About 18 pieces

⌾

Whether for a tea table or a dessert buffet, these tidbits, or bouchées, add interest to a selection of cookies or petits fours. Quickly assembled and quickly cooked, they are delicious.

2	tablespoons currants
3	tablespoons brandy or rum
2	cups unbleached flour, plus extra for shaping
1½	teaspoons baking powder
3	tablespoons granulated sugar
2	tablespoons (¼ stick) chilled unsalted butter, cubed
½	cup milk
1	large egg, well beaten
	Vegetable oil for frying or baking
	Confectioners' sugar for sprinkling

In a small bowl, mix the currants with the brandy or rum and let soak for 30 minutes.

Meanwhile, in a large bowl, sift together the flour, baking powder, and sugar. Cut in the butter with your fingers or 2 knives. In another small bowl, whisk together the milk and egg. Beat into the flour mixture. Drain the currants and stir them into the dough.

Turn the dough out onto a lightly floured surface. Using rounded tablespoons of dough, shape crescents with floured hands. When all are made, cover with a cloth and let rest 15 minutes.

To fry the crescents, fill a deep pan no more than halfway with oil, at least 2 inches, and bring it slowly to 375°F over moderate heat. Slide the crescents into the oil with a pancake turner, cooking 3 or 4 at a time. Turn the crescents with a slotted spoon and when golden brown on both sides, about 1½ minutes in all, lift out with a slotted spoon. Drain on paper towels and transfer to a rack over wax paper. Sprinkle with confectioners' sugar while still warm.

To bake the crescents, preheat the oven to 375°F. Place the crescents 1 inch apart on a parchment paper–lined baking sheet. Brush with oil and bake for 15 minutes, or until golden brown. Place on a rack over wax paper and sprinkle with confectioners' sugar.

Fresh Lemon Puffs

About 3 dozen pieces

⊂⊃

I *developed these delicacies from a favorite cake recipe. The resultant puffs are irregular globes of fresh lemon and almonds. They are best eaten the same day they are cooked.*

1 lemon
½ cup blanched almonds
½ cup sugar
3 large eggs
1½ cups unbleached flour
1 teaspoon baking powder
Vegetable oil for frying
½ cup sugar mixed with ½ teaspoon ground nutmeg

Peel the whole rind from the lemon including the white pith. Cut the peel in pieces, place in a small saucepan, and add water to cover. Boil for 20 minutes. Meanwhile, place the almonds and sugar in the bowl of a food processor and process until the mixture is ground to a powder.

Remove any seeds from the lemon and add the pulp to the sugar mixture in the processor. Drain the peel well and add also. Pulse the ingredients in the processor only until the peel is coarsely chopped but not pureed. Transfer the mixture to a large bowl.

Beat the eggs in the processor until frothy. Add the flour and baking powder and process briefly to mix. Return the lemon mixture to the processor and blend for no more than 5 seconds.

Fill a deep pan no more than halfway with oil, at least 2 inches, and bring it slowly to 375°F over moderate heat. Drop the dough by rounded teaspoons into the oil, using a second teaspoon dipped in the hot oil to push the dough off. Turn the puffs with a slotted spoon when the underside is golden brown, about 30 seconds. If the puff refuses to stay with its uncooked side down, use the slotted spoon to hold it in place briefly. From start to finish the puffs take only 1 minute to cook on average. Lift out the puffs with a slotted spoon and drain on paper towels. While still warm, shake the puffs in a paper bag with the sugar mixture.

FRITTERS

DRIED FRUIT FRITTERS
About 18 pieces

∽

The best dried fruits to make fritters with are
apricots, figs, and prunes. Any instructions on the package about soaking before stewing should be followed but
it is not necessary with most dried fruit. The batter
recipe may be doubled.

FRITTER BATTER

1	recipe apricots, figs, or prunes (recipes follow)
½	cup unbleached flour, plus ½ cup for coating
½	teaspoon baking powder
1	medium egg
6	tablespoons milk
½	tablespoon vegetable oil
1	medium egg white
	Vegetable oil for frying

Prepare one of the fruit recipes to cook in the fritters.

Into a medium-sized bowl or the bowl of an electric
mixer, sift the flour and baking powder. In another bowl,
whisk the egg with the milk, then add with the ½ tablespoon of oil to the bowl of the mixer. Beat together the
liquid mixture with the dry ingredients. In a medium-
sized bowl, beat the egg white until stiff but not dry, then
fold into the batter just before frying the prepared food.

Fill a deep pan no more than halfway with oil, at
least 2 inches, and bring it slowly to 375°F over moderate

heat. Sift the $^{1}/_{2}$ cup of flour onto a plate. Roll each piece of fruit in the flour and dip in the batter, letting any excess drip back into the bowl. Lower the fruit into the hot oil with a slotted spoon. Fry 3 or 4 pieces at a time and turn the fritters with a slotted spoon until they are golden brown on both sides, about $1^{1}/_{2}$ minutes in all. Lift out the fritters with a slotted spoon and drain on paper towels.

APRICOTS

18 dried apricots
 3 slices orange (optional)
 1 2-inch piece cinnamon stick (optional)
    Water to cover
    Fritter Batter

Place the apricots in a large saucepan with the orange slices or cinnamon stick, if used, and cover with water. Simmer, covered, for 40 to 45 minutes, or until tender. Drain and pat the apricots dry with paper towels. Proceed with the Dried Fruit Fritter recipe.

FIGS

18 dried figs, Mission type
    Water to cover
    Fritter Batter

Cover the figs with water and simmer, covered, in a large saucepan about 40 minutes, or until tender. Drain and pat the figs dry with paper towels. Proceed with the

Dried Fruit Fritter recipe. If desired, serve with sugar syrup (page 52), flavored with preserved ginger.

PRUNES

18 pitted prunes
2 slices lemon or orange
8 cloves
Water to cover
Fritter Batter
Confectioners' sugar

Place the prunes in a large saucepan with the slices of orange or lemon and the cloves. Cover with the water and simmer, covered, from 20 to 45 minutes, depending on how tender the dried prunes are. Drain and pat dry with paper towels. Proceed with the Dried Fruit Fritter recipe. Sprinkle with confectiponers' sugar to serve.

APPLE FRITTERS

About 16 pieces

∞

Since Roman times, fritter recipes have abounded. Almost any food can become a fritter when dipped in a batter or coated with egg and flour, then fried.

There are a few tips for successful fritter making: The food to be fried must be of uniform size and absolutely dry. The batter must be thick enough not to slide off the food.

The apples in this recipe may be cut in half-moon slices, as for apple pie, and the slices may be macerated in orange juice instead of brandy or cognac. This batter can be used for many other fruits, except those that follow with their own specific recipes.

4   apples, such as Golden Delicious or Rome
     Beauties
1   quart water
     Juice of 1 lemon
1/3   cup cognac or applejack brandy
1   cup unbleached flour, plus 1/2 cup for coating
1/2   teaspoon salt
2   large eggs
2   tablespoons vegetable oil
3/4   cup (6 ounces) beer
2   large egg whites
     Vegetable oil for frying
     Sugar for dredging

Peel and core the apples, leaving them whole. Cut $1/2$-inch slices across the apples, discarding the top and bottom slice. Drop the slices in the water with the lemon juice added to prevent them from turning brown. When all are cut, dry them with paper towels and macerate the slices with the cognac or brandy in a shallow platter for 30 minutes.

Sift the 1 cup of flour with the salt into a large bowl and the $1/2$ cup of flour onto a platter. Beat the eggs and oil together in a small bowl and stir in the beer. Beat the liquids into the large bowl of flour, cover, and set aside. Drain the apple slices, pat each slice dry, and dredge in the $1/2$ cup of flour. Just before using the batter, whisk the egg whites until stiff but not dry and fold gently into the batter.

Fill a deep pan no more than halfway with oil, at least 2 inches, and bring it slowly to 360°F. Dip each floured apple slice in the batter, letting any excess batter drip back into the bowl. Carefully slide each slice into the oil with your fingers, frying 3 or 4 slices at a time. Turn them with a slotted spoon when the underside is golden brown, about 1 minute. When both sides are golden brown, about 2 minutes in all, lift out with a slotted spoon and drain on paper towels. Transfer to a baking sheet lined with parchment paper and keep warm in a 250°F oven. When ready to serve, dredge the fritters with sugar.

Variation:

Use an equal amount of pears, apricots, or plums in place of the apples.

BANANA FRITTERS
About 28 pieces

∽

1 cup unbleached flour, plus $\frac{1}{2}$ cup for coating
1 teaspoon baking powder
2 tablespoons granulated sugar, divided
2 large eggs, separated
$\frac{1}{2}$ cup milk
1 tablespoon unsalted butter, melted
1 tablespoon plus $\frac{1}{2}$ cup light rum
4 large bananas, not too ripe
  Vegetable oil for frying
  Confectioners' sugar for sprinkling (optional)
  Caramel Glaze (optional)

Sift the 1 cup of flour, baking powder, and 1 tablespoon of the sugar into a large bowl. Make a well in the center and whisk in the egg yolks with the milk, mixing thoroughly. Beat in the butter and 1 tablespoon of the rum. Cover the bowl and set aside.

Peel the bananas and slice diagonally into $\frac{3}{4}$-inch pieces. Mix the $\frac{1}{2}$ cup of rum and the remaining tablespoon of sugar in a shallow platter. Macerate the banana pieces, turning them occasionally, for 1 hour. Sift the $\frac{1}{2}$ cup of flour onto a plate. Drain the slices and coat with flour. Set aside on wax paper.

Fill a deep pan no more than halfway with oil, at least 2 inches, and bring it slowly to 375°F over moderate heat. Meanwhile, whisk the egg whites until stiff but not dry, and gently fold into the batter until no trace of the whites remains. Dip each banana slice in the batter and carefully slide into the oil with your fingers, cooking 4 or 5 at a time. Turn the slices with a slotted spoon until golden brown on both sides, about 2 minutes in all. Lift out with a slotted spoon and drain on paper towels.

Serve hot, sprinkled with confectioners' sugar, if desired, or drizzled with Caramel Glaze.

CARAMEL GLAZE

    3 cups sugar
1 1/2 cups water

Combine the sugar and water in a heavy, medium-sized saucepan and cook, stirring, over low heat until the sugar is dissolved. Raise the heat and cook the syrup, without stirring, until it reaches 270°F or becomes light golden brown in color. Have a shallow pan of warm water nearby and put the pan of caramel into the water immediately. Keep the water in the shallow pan warm over medium-low heat until the fritters are ready.

CRANBERRY FRITTERS
About 20 pieces

⤫

I *was surprised to learn that the cranberry is not an American exclusive, but grows in most parts of the world. Too tart to eat raw, cranberries are wonderful in these fritters, which are perfect as a dessert for winter holiday feasts. They should be served hot, dredged with sugar and accompanied by a spoonful of crème fraîche or sour cream.*

 1   cup unbleached flour
 1   teaspoon baking powder
 1   tablespoon plus $1/3$ cup sugar
 2   large eggs, separated
 $3/4$ cup milk
 1   tablespoon vegetable oil
 $1/2$ teaspoon almond extract
 $1/3$ cup water
 2   cups cranberries, picked over
     Vegetable oil for frying
     Sugar for sprinkling
     Crème fraîche or sour cream

Sift the flour, baking powder, and 1 tablespoon of the sugar into a large bowl. In another bowl, whisk the egg yolks and the milk together. Beat the liquid mixture into the dry ingredients and stir in the oil and almond extract. Set aside, covered.

Bring the water and the ⅓ cup of sugar to boil over medium-high heat and add the cranberries immediately. Lower the heat and simmer until the cranberries burst, about 4 or 5 minutes. Drain the cranberries and spread them on a plate to cool. Just before frying the fritters, whisk the egg whites until stiff but not dry, and fold them gently into the batter. Do not overmix.

Fill a deep pan no more than halfway with oil, at least 2 inches, and bring it slowly to 370°F over moderate heat. Gently fold the cranberries into the batter. Using a 1-tablespoon measuring spoon, drop a heaping lump of batter into the oil, using another spoon dipped in the hot oil to push it off the spoon. Cook 3 or 4 fritters at a time, turning them over with a slotted spoon after they are golden brown on the underside, about 45 seconds. Move the pan to a cold burner if the temperature goes to 380°F, returning it to the heat when it descends to 360°F. The fritters fry very fast, about 1½ minutes in all. Some small morsels may break away from the main fritter. Turn them also and lift out all bits after removing the fritters with a slotted spoon to drain on paper towels.

Keep the fritters hot on a parchment paper–lined baking sheet in a 250°F oven. Serve the fritters when all are fried, sprinkled with sugar and with crème fraîche or sour cream on the side.

Variation: **BLUEBERRY FRITTERS**

Fold 2 cups of uncooked blueberries into the batter instead of cranberries. To serve, sprinkle the fritters with brown sugar, if desired. These fritters may also be cooked on a griddle like pancakes.

ELDERFLOWER FRITTERS
About 8 pieces

∞

These lovely and common flowers can be trans-
formed into an uncommon and decorative dessert.
They are lacy and appetizing served on a puree of
strawberries or blueberries, or simply powdered with
confectioners' sugar. These were a feature of banquets in
the French Middle Ages. Make sure that the flowers
have not been sprayed with chemicals.

1½   cups unbleached flour
½   cup cornstarch
1   large egg, separated
¾   cup white wine
¾   cup water
    Pinch of salt (optional)
8   elderflower blossoms
    Vegetable oil for frying
1   pint strawberries or blueberries, washed and
    pureed (optional)
    Confectioners' sugar (optional)

Sift the flour and cornstarch into a large bowl. In
another bowl, whisk the egg yolk with the wine, water,
and salt, if used. Slowly beat into the flour mixture. Put
through a sieve, if necessary, to remove any lumps. Cover
and set aside for 30 minutes.

Meanwhile, dip the flowers briefly into a bowl of
tepid water and dry with paper towels. Trim off the

stems, leaving just enough to hold with a pair of tongs for dipping into the batter.

Fill a deep pan no more than halfway with oil, at least 2 inches, and bring it slowly to 360°F over moderate heat. Beat the egg whites until stiff but not dry, and fold into the batter just before frying. Dip a blossom into the batter, holding the stem with a pair of tongs. Plunge immediately into the oil. Fry 1 blossom at a time, turning with a slotted spoon until golden brown, about 1 minute in all. Lift out with a slotted spoon to drain on paper towels. Carefully monitor the temperature of the oil by moving the pan to a cold burner when the temperature rises to 375°F. Repeat frying the flowers, one at a time, and serve while still warm with the fruit puree or confectioners' sugar.

SQUASH BLOSSOM FRITTERS
About 12 pieces

∽

One of early summer's most fleeting pleasures, these edible flowers are worth a party. I make them as a first course or to accompany chili con carne. The heartiness of the chili complements the delicacy of the fritters. You must make sure that the flowers have not been sprayed with chemicals.

The fritters must be prepared, fried, and served in a twinkling.

12   squash blossoms, trimmed of stems and pistils
²⁄₃   cup farmer cheese or large curd cottage cheese
  2   tablespoons honey
       Pinch of ground nutmeg
  1   teaspoon grated lemon zest
½   cup unbleached flour
  2   tablespoons cornstarch
  2   large eggs, separated
       Vegetable oil for frying

Dip the blossoms in a bowl of tepid water and pat thoroughly dry with paper towels. Press the farmer or cottage cheese through a sieve and whisk in a large bowl with the honey, nutmeg, and lemon zest. Sift the flour and cornstarch together in a medium-sized bowl. Beat the egg yolks in a medium-sized bowl. Beat the egg whites until stiff but not dry, and fold into the yolks.

Insert a generous teaspoon of the cheese mixture into each blossom, closing the petals over the filling.

Fill a deep pan no more than halfway with oil, at least 2 inches, and bring it slowly to 360°F over moderate heat. Roll the blossoms in the flour mixture, then dip them into the eggs, preparing 2 or 3 at a time and placing them on wax paper. Lift the flowers into the oil with a slotted spoon, turning with a slotted spoon until both sides are golden brown and crisp, about 1½ minutes in all. Lift the fritters out with a slotted spoon and drain on paper towels.

OTHER DELIGHTS

ROSETTES

About 4 dozen pieces

∽

Although *rosette irons and the delicate pastries they make are often considered Scandinavian specialties, the Italians also use them to turn out crisp treats in a flash. Children adore helping to make these instantaneous goodies. Be sure to read carefully the instructions that accompany your iron before using it.*

2 large eggs
1 cup milk
  Pinch of salt
1 teaspoon granulated sugar
1 cup unbleached flour
  Vegetable oil for frying
  Confectioners' sugar for sprinkling

Whisk together the eggs, milk, salt, and sugar. Gradually whisk in the flour. Let the batter stand, covered, for 30 minutes.

Fill a deep pan no more than halfway with oil, at least 3 inches, and bring it slowly to 355°F over moderate heat. Heat the iron by dipping it into the hot oil and letting any excess drip back into the pan, then quickly dip the iron into the batter and plunge it back into the oil. Almost immediately the rosette will puff and then it can be eased off the iron with a fork. The rosette will become golden in seconds. Lift out with a slotted spoon to drain on paper towels. Remove to a rack over wax paper and sprinkle with confectioners' sugar.

HONEY CINNAMON FRIED BREAD
About 8 pieces

∽

Years ago, in New York, I worked briefly with a restaurant whose busiest hour was teatime. The clientele, mostly blue-haired matrons, ate only one specialty: slices of challah bread, dipped in soft black-cherry ice cream and fried in butter! An uptown version of French toast?

8   slices day-old Italian bread, ¾ inch thick
1   cup half-and-half or light cream
⅓   cup honey
1   cinnamon stick
    Vegetable oil for frying or baking
2   large eggs
1   cup sugar mixed with 1 tablespoon ground
       cinnamon

Arrange the bread in a single layer in a shallow baking pan. Combine the half-and-half or cream, honey, and cinnamon stick in a medium-sized saucepan and bring to a boil over medium-high heat. Lower the heat and simmer for 10 minutes. Pour the mixture over the bread, removing the cinnamon stick, and let the bread soak for 2 or 3 minutes. Transfer the bread to a wire rack placed over a baking pan or dish and let it dry for at least 2 hours.

To fry the bread, bring 1 inch of oil to 360°F over moderate heat in a deep skillet or sauté pan. Lightly beat the eggs in a shallow dish. Dip each slice of bread in the beaten eggs and fry in the oil until golden brown, turning only once, about 1 minute each side. Place the sugar mixture on a plate and coat both sides of each slice. Serve immediately, 2 slices to each person. Alternately, brush each slice with the sugar mixture.

To bake the bread, preheat the oven to 375°F. Dip only one side of bread in the beaten eggs and place the bread with the egg side up on an oiled baking sheet. Bake for 15 minutes, or until golden brown. Sprinkle with the sugar mixture and serve warm, or slide under the broiler to melt the sugar slightly. You may also brush the bread with the sugar mixture.

Fried Sweet Dough

About 2 dozen pieces

Whether they are fried or baked, you will love these spicy morsels. They could qualify as fast food, so easily are they tossed together and just as quickly consumed. Perfect for Halloween parties or to accompany Christmas eggnog.

1¾ cups unbleached flour
1 teaspoon baking powder
½ teaspoon baking soda
¼ teaspoon ground nutmeg
¼ teaspoon ground cinnamon
¼ teaspoon ground ginger
1 large egg
½ cup sugar
6 tablespoons buttermilk
2 tablespoons vegetable oil
Vegetable oil for frying or baking
1 cup sugar for sprinkling

Sift the flour, baking powder, baking soda, nutmeg, cinnamon, and ginger into a large bowl. Whisk the egg with the sugar and buttermilk in another bowl. Make a well in the flour mixture and beat in the liquid mixture with the 2 tablespoons of oil. Turn the dough out onto a floured surface and knead lightly several times. Roll tablespoons of dough into balls. Place them on a towel or wax paper, covered with a cloth, until all are shaped.

To fry the balls, fill a deep pan no more than halfway with oil, at least 2 inches, and bring it to 360°F over moderate heat. Carefully lower the balls into the oil with a slotted spoon, cooking 3 or 4 at a time, and turn them with a slotted spoon until all sides are golden brown and puffed, about 3 minutes in all. Drain on paper towels and shake in a paper bag with the sugar, or place on a rack over wax paper and sprinkle with the sugar while warm.

To bake the balls, preheat the oven to 375°F. Place the balls 1 inch apart on a greased baking sheet and bake for 15 minutes, or until golden brown. Place on a rack over wax paper, brush with additional oil, and sprinkle with sugar.

HAND PIES
About 8 pieces

The term hand pies *comes from the Pennsylvania Dutch tradition of turnovers carried by the farmers to the fields, or children to school, both for sustenance and to keep their hands warm. Smaller pies, which I call "finger pies," are my own invention for parties. Instead of the customary meat-based fillings, these pies have fruit or vegetable mixtures inside.*

PASTRY

- 3 cups unbleached flour, plus extra for rolling out and cutting
- 1/2 teaspoon salt
- 1/2 cup (1 stick) unsalted butter, chilled
- 1/2 cup (1 stick) unsalted margarine, chilled
- 1/2 cup ice water, plus more as needed

APPLE AND PARSNIP FILLING

- 1 pound apples, such as Granny Smith
- 1 cup sugar
- 1/2 cup water
- 2 pounds parsnips, peeled
- 1/4 cup (1/2 stick) unsalted butter or margarine, softened
- 1/2 teaspoon freshly ground pepper
- 1 egg beaten with 1 tablespoon cream for the glaze

To make the pastry, place the flour, salt, butter, and margarine in a large bowl or the bowl of a food processor. Cut the ingredients together using 2 knives, your fingers, or the steel blade of a food processor until crumbly. Sprinkle $\frac{1}{2}$ cup of the ice water over the mixture and blend just until the dough can be gathered into a ball, adding more water drop by drop, if necessary. Wrap in plastic wrap and chill for at least an hour.

To make the Apple and Parsnip Filling, core the unpeeled apples and cut in eighths. In a large, heavy saucepan, mix the sugar and $\frac{1}{2}$ cup water. Stir over moderate heat until the sugar is dissolved. Bring to a boil over medium-high heat and cook, stirring, for 2 minutes, then remove from the heat. Stir in the apples and let simmer over low heat. Cook until soft, about 10 minutes. Puree with the liquid mixture in a food processor or pass through a food mill. Set aside.

Cut the parsnips into 1-inch pieces and place in a large, heavy saucepan. Cover with water and boil, covered, until soft, about 20 minutes. Drain the parsnips and put through a food mill while still warm. Beat in the butter and pepper. Mix thoroughly with the apple puree and cool.

To assemble the pies, roll out half the dough to a $\frac{1}{8}$-inch thickness, refrigerating the other half. For hand pies use a 6-inch saucer as a guide to cut 4 rounds, or for finger pies, a 3-inch cutter to cut 9 rounds. Repeat with the second half of the pastry. Have ready a cup of cold water, a $\frac{1}{2}$-cup measuring cup for hand pies or a tablespoon for finger pies, and the cooled filling.

Moisten halfway around the edge of the round with the water. Place $\frac{1}{2}$ cup of filling slightly off center toward the moist edge of the pastry for hand pies, a heaping tablespoon for finger pies. Fold the dough over the filling to make a half circle and crimp the edges with a fork. Chill the pies for 30 minutes.

To fry the pies, bring 1½ inches of oil to 370°F in a deep pan over moderate heat. Lower the pies into the oil with a spatula, frying 2 or 3 pies at a time, turning with a slotted spoon until golden brown, about 4 minutes in all. Drain on paper towels.

To bake the pies, preheat the oven to 375°F. Place the pies on an ungreased or parchment paper–lined baking sheet. Brush them with the egg wash and bake until golden brown, about 20 to 25 minutes for hand pies and about 15 to 20 minutes for finger pies.

Variation: **Sweet Potato Filling**

3	pounds (4 to 5 large) sweet potatoes
1	cup brown sugar, firmly packed
2	cups light cream or evaporated milk
1	teaspoon ground ginger
1	teaspoon ground nutmeg
½	teaspoon ground cloves
½	teaspoon salt
¼	cup vegetable oil or unsalted butter, melted

Preheat the oven to 400°F. Scrub the potatoes but do not peel. Bake in a shallow baking pan 45 minutes to 1 hour, or until tender. Split the potatoes while still hot and scrape out the pulp. Place in the bowl of a food processor with the remaining ingredients and pulse until smooth, or mash by hand. Let cool.

Variation: **CARROT AND RAISIN FILLING**

>   1 cup golden raisins
>   ¼ cup light rum
>   2 pounds carrots, peeled and grated
>   1 cup grated white cabbage
>   1 cup mayonnaise
>   1 teaspoon ground cinnamon

Soak the raisins in the rum in a small bowl for 30 minutes. Pat the grated carrots dry with paper towels and mix thoroughly with the cabbage in a large bowl. Combine the raisins and rum with the vegetables. Add the mayonnaise and cinnamon, and mix thoroughly.

Variation: **GUAVA PASTE WITH COCONUT**

>   8 ounces guava paste (available in most
>   supermarkets and specialty shops)
>   1 cup quick-cooking tapioca
>   2 cups milk
>   2 cups unsweetened coconut flakes
>   1 tablespoon grated orange zest

Chop the guava paste as fine as possible and combine in a heavy, medium-sized saucepan with the tapioca and milk. Let stand for 5 minutes, then bring to a boil over low heat, stirring the mixture constantly, about 3 to 4 minutes, or until it thickens. Remove from the heat and stir in the coconut and orange zest. Let cool.

SWEET HUSH PUPPIES
About 30 pieces

∞

My family's "authentic" Southern hush puppies were made with yellow cornmeal. However, the yellow cornmeal available in supermarkets seems to have changed in the last fifty years. I have difficulty keeping the little balls from separating in the hot oil, and white cornmeal works better for me today. These are favorites with crisp bacon or fried country ham.

- 2 cups stone-ground white cornmeal
- 2 tablespoons sugar
- 1 teaspoon baking soda
- 2 large eggs
- 1 cup buttermilk
  Vegetable oil for frying
  Maple syrup

Sift together the cornmeal, sugar, and baking soda into a medium-sized bowl. In another bowl, whisk together the eggs and buttermilk until foamy. Beat the liquid into the dry ingredients and set aside, covered, for 30 minutes.

Fill a deep pan no more than halfway with oil, at least 2 inches, and bring it slowly to 375°F over moderate heat. Take generous teaspoonfuls of batter, and use another teaspoon dipped in the hot oil to push the batter into the oil, cooking 3 or 4 hush puppies at a time. Turn the hush puppies with a slotted spoon until golden brown on all sides, about 2 minutes in all. Lift out with a slotted spoon and drain on paper towels. Keep hot in a 200°F oven on a parchment paper–lined baking sheet. Serve as soon as all are fried, with maple syrup warmed over low heat.

Peanut Butter Fingers

About 24 pieces

∾

These flaky tidbits melt in the mouth and are perfect to serve with drinks, whether cider or slightly chilled wine. They can be baked as tartlet shells, and when filled with jelly, they are a very grown-up version of peanut butter-and-jelly sandwiches. The recipe can be doubled or tripled.

- ¾ cup unbleached flour, plus extra for rolling out and cutting
  Pinch of salt
- 2 tablespoons unsalted butter, chilled and cubed
- 2 tablespoons unsalted margarine, chilled and cubed
- 6 tablespoons peanut butter, either smooth or crunchy
- 3 tablespoons ice water, or as needed
  Vegetable oil for frying
  Jam or jelly for filling (optional)

Sift the flour and salt into a medium-sized bowl or the bowl of a food processor. With your fingertips, 2 knives, or the steel blade of the processor, cut in the butter and margarine until the mixture resembles oatmeal. Blend in the peanut butter. Slowly add the ice water until the dough forms a ball. Turn the dough out onto a lightly floured surface and knead lightly 3 or 4 times. Pat into a disk 1 inch thick, wrap in plastic wrap, and refrigerate for 1 hour.

On a floured surface roll out the pastry between $\frac{1}{8}$ and $\frac{1}{4}$ inch thick. Cut in strips $\frac{1}{2}$ inch wide and $2\frac{1}{2}$ to 3 inches long. Set the strips aside and cover with a cloth.

To fry the fingers, bring $1\frac{1}{2}$ inches of oil in a deep pan to 340°F over moderate heat. With a spatula, slip the strips into the oil, cooking 3 or 4 at a time. Remember to control the temperature, moving the pan to a cold burner if the temperature rises to 360°F. The fingers are very fragile and take about 45 seconds for each side to turn golden brown. Turn the strips with a slotted spoon and when both sides are golden brown, about $1\frac{1}{2}$ minutes in all, lift out with a slotted spoon and drain on paper towels. Cool on a rack.

To bake the fingers, preheat the oven to 400°F. Place the strips 1 inch apart on a parchment paper–lined baking sheet and bake for 10 to 15 minutes or until golden brown. Alternately, press the dough into small tartlet pans and bake in a preheated 375°F oven for 10 minutes, or until golden brown. Turn out to cool on a rack and fill with jelly or jam, or as desired.

LOW-FAT, LOW-CHOLESTEROL DOUGHNUTS

Chocolate Low-Fat, Low-Cholesterol Doughnuts

About 12 pieces

✣

Although not a perfect facsimile of my chocolate doughnut recipe on page 33, these make a satisfying substitute. It is difficult to judge the doneness of the frying doughnuts because of the dark color of the dough, therefore the timing is even more important than usual. As with the Low-Cholesterol Apple-Yogurt Doughnuts (page 91), baking will not be successful because of the low-fat content, and the low 350 °F frying temperature is crucial.

½	cup pitted prunes
½	cup sugar
1¾	cups cake flour
1	teaspoon baking powder
3	tablespoons unsweetened cocoa
2	large egg whites
	Vegetable oil for frying

Place the prunes in a small, heavy saucepan and add enough water to barely cover the prunes. Bring to a simmer over moderate heat. When the prunes are soft and slightly puffed, about 15 minutes, drain off any remaining liquid without pressing out any water absorbed by the fruit. Place the prunes in a food processor and puree with the sugar, or pass the prunes through a food mill and stir in the sugar. Sift the flour, baking powder, and cocoa into a large bowl. Stir in the puree and set aside. Whisk the egg whites in another bowl until they form soft peaks and stir into the dough with a rubber spatula until thoroughly incorporated.

Turn out the dough onto a floured surface and pat into a round of ½-inch thickness with floured hands. Cut out doughnuts with a doughnut cutter. Reroll the dough including the holes and cut additional doughnuts until all the dough is used.

Fill a deep pan no more than halfway with oil, at least 2 inches, and bring it slowly to 350°F over moderate heat. With a floured pancake turner, slide the doughnuts into the oil, cooking 2 at a time. After 1 minute, turn with a slotted spoon and cook the second side for just 1 minute, or until puffed, but do not cook for more than 5 seconds past a minute. Lift out with a slotted spoon to drain on paper towels. Cool on a rack.

LOW-CHOLESTEROL APPLE-YOGURT DOUGHNUTS

About 20 pieces

∞

After many different experimental recipes and dozens of rubbery doughnuts, these apple and yogurt ones evolved. The yogurt tenderizes the gluten in the unbleached flour and the applesauce provides fiber and viscosity. These doughnuts are chewy rather than light because of the absence of fat and eggs, but delicious nevertheless. Baking renders these doughnuts disagreeably tough and is not recommended.

I adapted the ingredients from an article by Marian Burros in the New York Times, which was inspired by Harold McGee's book On Food and Cooking (Scribner's, 1984).

$1\frac{1}{2}$ cups unbleached flour, plus extra for rolling out
     and cutting
1   cup cake flour
1   cup granulated sugar
1   teaspoon baking soda
1   teaspoon cinnamon
$\frac{1}{2}$ teaspoon ground nutmeg
$\frac{1}{2}$ teaspoon ground cloves
1   apple such as Golden Delicious, peeled, cored,
     and coarsely chopped
$\frac{2}{3}$ cup low-fat yogurt
     Vegetable oil for frying
     Confectioners' sugar (optional)

Sift together the unbleached flour, cake flour, sugar, baking soda, cinnamon, nutmeg, and cloves into a large bowl. Place the apple in a small, heavy saucepan and add enough water to barely cover. Cook over medium heat until very soft, about 15 minutes. Drain the apple and mix with the yogurt.

Stir the apple mixture into the dry ingredients until well combined. Turn the dough out onto a floured surface and knead with floured hands, adding additional flour if the dough is too sticky. Pat out to a $1/2$-inch thickness and let rest, covered with a towel, for 15 minutes. Cut out doughnuts with a floured doughnut cutter and cover doughnuts with a cloth. Reroll the dough and holes and cut additional doughnuts until all the dough is used.

Fill a deep pan no more than halfway with oil, at least 2 inches, and bring to exactly 350°F over moderate heat. The temperature of the oil is crucial because I found that at 360°F or higher the interior did not have time to cook before the exterior was brown. Slide the doughnuts into the oil with a floured pancake turner, cooking 2 or 3 at a time. Turn the doughnuts with a slotted spoon when the bottom side is golden brown, about $1 1/4$ minutes. Lift the doughnuts out with a slotted spoon when both sides are golden brown, about $2 1/2$ minutes in all. Maintain a temperature of 350°F as closely as possible by moving the pan between the heat and a cold burner. Drain the doughnuts on paper towels and transfer to a rack over wax paper. Sprinkle with confectioners' sugar, if desired.

ACKNOWLEDGMENTS

I owe thanks to Katie Workman and Pam Krauss,
my editors, for their infinite patience and advice. I am
also grateful for the courageous appetites
of all my family and friends.

INDEX

CONVERSION CHART

EQUIVALENT IMPERIAL AND METRIC MEASUREMENTS

American cooks use standard containers, the 8-ounce cup and a tablespoon that takes exactly 16 level fillings to fill that cup level. Measuring by cup makes it very difficult to give weight equivalents, as a cup of densely packed butter will weigh considerably more than a cup of flour. The easiest way therefore to deal with cup measurements in recipes is to take the amount by volume rather than by weight. Thus the equation reads:

1 cup = 240 ml = 8 fl. oz. $\frac{1}{2}$ cup = 120 ml = 4 fl. oz.

It is possible to buy a set of American cup measures in major stores around the world. In the States, butter is often measured in sticks. One stick is the equivalent of 8 tablespoons. One tablespoon of butter is therefore the equivalent to $\frac{1}{2}$ ounce/15 grams.

LINEAR MEASURES

1 inch	2.54 centimeters
1 foot	0.3048 meters

LIQUID MEASURES

Fluid ounces	U.S. measures	Imperial measures	Milliliters
	1 TSP	1 TSP	5
$\frac{1}{4}$	2 TSP	1 DESSERTSPOON	7
$\frac{1}{2}$	1 TBS	1 TBS	15
1	2 TBS	2 TBS	28
2	$\frac{1}{4}$ CUP	4 TBS	56
4	$\frac{1}{2}$ CUP OR $\frac{1}{4}$ PINT		110
5		$\frac{1}{4}$ PINT OR 1 GILL	140
6	$\frac{3}{4}$ CUP		170
8	1 CUP OR $\frac{1}{2}$ PINT		225
9			250, $\frac{1}{4}$ LITER
10	$1\frac{1}{4}$ CUPS	$\frac{1}{2}$ PINT	280
12	$1\frac{1}{2}$ CUPS	$\frac{3}{4}$ PINT	340
15	$\frac{3}{4}$ PINT		420
16	2 CUPS OR 1 PINT		450
18	$2\frac{1}{4}$ CUPS		500, $\frac{1}{2}$ LITER
20	$2\frac{1}{2}$ CUPS	1 PINT	560
24	3 CUPS OR $1\frac{1}{2}$ PINTS		675
25		$1\frac{1}{4}$ PINTS	700
27	$3\frac{1}{2}$ CUPS		750
30	$3\frac{3}{4}$ CUPS	$1\frac{1}{2}$ PINTS	840
32	4 CUPS OR 2 PINTS OR 1 QUART		900
35		$1\frac{3}{4}$ PINTS	980
36	$4\frac{1}{2}$ CUPS		1000, 1 LITER
40	5 CUPS OR $2\frac{1}{2}$ PINTS	2 PINTS OR 1 QUART	1120

SOLID MEASURES

U.S. and Imperial Measures		Metric Measures	
OUNCES	POUNDS	GRAMS	KILOS
1		28	
2		56	
$3\frac{1}{2}$		100	
4	$\frac{1}{4}$	112	
5		140	
6		168	
8	$\frac{1}{2}$	225	
9		250	$\frac{1}{4}$
12	$\frac{3}{4}$	340	
16	1	450	
18		500	$\frac{1}{2}$
20	$1\frac{1}{4}$	560	
24	$1\frac{1}{2}$	675	
27		750	$\frac{3}{4}$
28	$1\frac{3}{4}$	780	
32	2	900	
36	$2\frac{1}{4}$	1000	1
40	$2\frac{1}{2}$	1100	
48	3	1350	
54		1500	$1\frac{1}{2}$
64	4	1800	
72	$4\frac{1}{2}$	2000	2
80	5	2250	$2\frac{1}{4}$
90		2500	$2\frac{1}{2}$
100	6	2800	$2\frac{3}{4}$

SUGGESTED EQUIVALENTS AND SUBSTITUTES FOR INGREDIENTS

all-purpose flour—plain flour
confectioners' sugar—icing sugar
cornstarch—cornflour
granulated sugar—caster sugar
shortening—white fat
unbleached flour—strong, white flour
vanilla bean—vanilla pod
zest—rind
light cream—single cream
heavy cream—double cream
half and half—12% fat milk
buttermilk—ordinary milk
sour milk—add 1 TBS vinegar or lemon juice to 1 cup minus 1 TBS lukewarm milk. Let stand for 5 minutes.
cheesecloth—muslin

OVEN TEMPERATURE EQUIVALENTS

Fahrenheit	Celsius	Gas Mark	Description
225	110	$\frac{1}{4}$	Cool
250	130	$\frac{1}{2}$	
275	140	1	Very Slow
300	150	2	
325	170	3	Slow
350	180	4	Moderate
375	190	5	
400	200	6	Moderately Hot
425	220	7	Fairly Hot
450	230	8	Hot
475	240	9	Very Hot
500	250	10	Extremely Hot

Any broiling recipes can be used with the grill of the oven, but beware of high-temperature grills.